ANGER

MANAGEMENT

EXERCISES

Know and control your "anger" type

Shunsuke Ando

Anger Management Exercises
- Know and control your "anger" type -
© Shunsuke Ando 2020
First Published in Japan in 2016 by Discover 21, Inc.

ISBN: 978-1-64273-096-8

Written by Shunsuke Ando
Book Designed by Lamplighters Label

Printed in USA
1 2 3 4 5 6 7 8 9 10

43-32 22nd Street STE 204 Long Island City New York 11101
www.onepeacebooks.com

Foreword

It's 8:00AM and you're walking to work. Suddenly you notice a person looking at their smartphone approaching from the opposite direction. You only have time to grunt before they smash into you – eyes still glued to their phone. They say nothing, and just keep walking. How do you feel? Do you indignantly yell out, "Watch where you're going!"? Do you figure that it's not worth getting upset about?

There are two types of people in the world: people who get angry over breaches of etiquette, and people who don't. Those who care about violations like these may get annoyed whenever they encounter people who "break the rules." From the perspective of people who don't care, these may seem like minor issues that should be easy to overlook, but that isn't always the case for everyone. What accounts for the difference? It all comes down to your emotional habits.

Anger habits

What are "emotional habits"? The dictionary describes "habit" as "a settled or regular tendency or practice." Anger is an emotion too, and "anger habits" describe those situations in which you have a tendency to get angry, or the ways in which you get angry. Things that greatly influence these anger habits include your worldview and expectations. For example, perhaps you see humans as fundamentally virtuous or you seem them as fundamentally depraved. Perhaps you are the type to be very prudent, or the type to dive into something without a plan. It's hard for us to notice our habits when it comes to the things that frustrate us – and regardless of whether we're conscious of these habits or not, they're difficult to fix.

That said, everyone has anger habits. They aren't a problem in themselves. They're only a problem if they lead you to hurt yourself or the people around you. For a long time, I hated my own anger habits but felt helpless to change them. I was constantly worried about it. I would always ask myself why this or that made me so angry. I wanted to never feel controlled by my anger again. I wanted to feel free from anger. I had these thoughts every day.

Anger management changed my life!

A turning point eventually came for me. I encountered anger management, and it changed my life. In 2003, while I was living in New York, I started attending anger management lectures at the recommendation of a friend. I remember thinking, "This is so easy, even I could do it!"

All of the methods for addressing anger that I had encountered in the past were spirituality-based. Many of them involved statements like, "Make a determination not to get angry," or, "No matter what happens, find the good in others." I couldn't help but think that if it was that easy, I wouldn't be struggling so much! This form of anger management is a systematized approach for mental education and mental training. It's easily accessible to men and women of all ages.

Anger management was developed in the US, but is strongly influenced by Eastern philosophy. Perhaps this background was the reason that I, as a person of East Asian descent, was able to grasp the principles of anger management so quickly.

The method was easy to understand and the content was just plain interesting. I got increasingly hooked on anger management and greedily built up my training with a variety of teachers. Anger management is not something that you slowly get better at day by day. As you continue, you suddenly have days where things that used to bother you no longer bother you and things you used to notice are no longer so apparent. As these experiences build, you progress.

Take the smartphone example mentioned above – even if today you absolutely can't tolerate that sort of thing, eventually there would come a day when it didn't bother you anymore. In my case, my relationships with my parents – my father in particular – got dramatically better. I used to have no patience when my father tried to lecture me, but one day it simply stopped upsetting me – as though I had crossed some boundary.

Hearing things from him that once made me think, "Why do you have to get so hung up on everything?" instead made me think, "Oh, you're saying that because you're worried." This was a breakthrough for me. The stress from my relationship with my father once had a major negative effect on me. Now that it has changed, my work and domestic life has changed for the better as well.

It was around this time that I quit my job to start my own business. I remember that it was a stressful time for me in terms of career. I am absolutely certain that I was only able to deal with my stress and get my business on track because I took my lessons to heart and learned to control my anger.

Anger can be controlled!

I expect everyone who has this book in their hands has, at the very least, some doubts and concerns about their own anger or the people around them. "Why do I get so angry over something like this? Why does that person always get so annoyed? I don't want to get so upset anymore. I don't want to get irritated over little things…." However, there may be quite a few of you who think that anger is difficult to control.

The difficulty arises from the need for people to understand their "anger habits." Without that understanding, there is no way to help the situation.

For example, somebody who isn't aware that they fidget will have no way of fixing the habit until somebody points it out to them. There's this question of whether or not people can become aware of their habits – but it's a simple matter. Using this book, you can come to understand your own "anger habits." By attaining this understanding, it will be possible to change behavior that has a negative effect on yourself and others.

If anger habits can be changed, controlling anger becomes easy (and without knowing one's anger habits, trying to control one's anger is like going to sea without a sextant). This book helps you diagnose your anger habits and type and offers you a method for dealing with those habits effectively. What kinds of anger habits do you have? To what should you pay attention, and what should you do? This book lays it all out clearly for you.

Your anger type is your sextant, and it shows you your path to controlling your anger. With such a tool, you can learn to not be blown around by your feelings of irritability. I hope you use this book to get your tools in hand and strike out on a journey towards a better life.

I'm confident that you'll find the journey to be a pleasant one.

table of contents

CHAPTER 4 | A 21-DAY CONSTITUTION TRAINING PROGRAM TO LEARN ANGER MANAGEMENT 111

Chapter 1

"Anger-Prone Personalities" Can Be Changed!

Is being "prone to anger" an incurable personality trait?

"Anger" is an emotional habit.
By understanding this, change is possible.

As the Japanese saying goes, "People have 48 habits for every 7 they don't." Pen-twirling, nail-biting, touching your face. Talking to yourself, pet phrases. What kinds of habits do you have?

As it happens, we have emotional habits as well. "Emotional habits" describes our tendency towards certain emotions and difficulty with others. That is to say, there are certain emotions we frequently "use" and certain emotions we frequently do not use.

What kind of emotions do you tend to feel? Do you get angry often? Or do you feel happy often? Or maybe you feel sad a lot?

Try taking a look around you. What kinds of emotional habits do the people around you have? Do they tend to get angry? Are they always smiling? Do they tend to be saddened by things, or find everything amusing? You can probably identify quite a few personality types.

However, while you may think that people who are quick to anger are fundamentally like that, it's not necessarily true. They may just be getting angry as a matter of habit.

Habits like the pen-twirling or nail-biting examples above are relatively easy for a person to realize and become open to feedback from people around them.

However, emotional habits cannot be identified at a glance, and are difficult for the habit owner to recognize. It's a sad state of affairs when others continue to suffer for as long as a person doesn't recognize their flaw.

But would someone be able to do anything about their habit even if they recognized it?

Are "emotional habits" decided at birth?

Emotional habits are acquired in childhood. If a child is frequently exposed to anger, they tend to be prone to anger themselves in adulthood.

When a fawn falls, it is able to pick itself back up right away. Within a few hours, it can stand on its own feet and walk around. Without being able to walk on their own, they would be targeted by predators and quickly die. This risk doesn't change, regardless of whether the parent deer are around or not.

Humans don't need to be able to stand up on their own immediately after birth, let alone walk. Parents do everything they can to protect their child.

Humans live for a very long time and learn a great many things. This is true of both factual knowledge and emotional expression. We learn our emotional expressions from our parents. To a child, their parents are the world, and imitate their parents in order to enter that world.

If a child encounters the emotion "anger" most as a child, anger is the emotion that will come most naturally to them when they become adults. When children encounter "joy" the most as a child, "joy" is the emotion that they are most capable of communicating when telling somebody something.

This isn't a matter of what's good or bad, but simply the nature of imprinting, which results in the emotion with highest exposure being the easiest to use. In this way, a person's emotional habits tend to follow those of their family.

When you were a child and a parent got mad at you, or you saw them get angry, did you ever think to yourself, "I'm never going to let myself get angry like that"?

Did you ever end up discovering – to your horror and astonishment – that the anger that you hated as a child had become the very same anger you express as an adult?

When I was a child, I hated it when I was asked angrily, "Why can't you do this?!" In my heart, I thought that asking me "Why?" doesn't do any good – if I can't do it, I can't do it! As a result, I was determined to never get mad like that as an adult – and I was terrified when I came to realize that I have engaged in the exact same sort of furious cross-examination myself.

People with children may even wonder to themselves, "Where did they learn to talk like that?!" – only to realize that their children get angry in the exact same way they do.

"Why?" "You should know better!" "Fine, whatever!" Speech habits often include extreme phrases like this.

If "emotional habits" are all flaws, should they be fixed?

Emotional habits become flaws if they're difficult to manage. That can be fixed!

However, should *all* "emotional habits" be fixed? You may have a negative association with the word "habit."

If you are able to manage your emotions well, that's a virtue, and doesn't need fixing. Conversely, if it's not so easy to manage them, it's a flaw.

For example, let's say there is a person with a habit towards anger that manifests as a "strong sense of justice." In general, a strong sense of justice seems like it could be a virtue.

Maybe you get annoyed at people with bad manners, or feel fury towards unscrupulous politicians. Thinking this way is good, and may be the proper way for humans to be.

But what happens if that sense of justice is too strong? For example, maybe you warn people who are being impolite. That's fine, but if you spend your entire day bitterly complaining – "I ran into nothing but assholes again today. It really pisses me off!" – that's a problem.

To take it to a further extreme, if you can't get someone to stop by talking to them, you may try to stop them by force. At this point, there's a big problem.

I believe that human emotional habits can be a virtue when properly managed, and vices when not. Those *vices* can be fixed.

Anger is the only emotion that can ruin your life

Once you understand the principles of anger management, it'll be easy for you to deal with feelings of anger.

It is very important to understand emotional habits, and anger habits in particular. This is because anger is the only emotion that can ruin your life.

Have you ever damaged a relationship of many years from just a single word in anger, or just one unnecessary comment?

I've heard of employees who stop coming to work after being yelled at once for some trivial error.

It's the same in private life. Maybe you've viscerally felt decades of trust start to break apart between you and your wife because of something stupid you said in a big fight.

I mentioned this before, but it's difficult for us to recognize our own emotional habits. By using the anger management diagnostic test in this book, you can learn your habits in an objective way.

Once seeing the result, many people will likely find that they agree with it. "Ahhh – so that's what it was." Maybe you'll learn about some side of yourself you had been avoiding.

Stay brave, and stand ready to face your anger habits. By confronting these difficult truths and following the anger management training, you will become able to manage your feelings.

You can change – from someone who is pushed around by and gives in to their anger, to someone who uses their anger as a source of energy to live in a more positive way.

Getting angry isn't the problem!
(What is the goal of anger management?)

The goal of anger management is to attain a state in which you get angry when it's appropriate, but don't get angry for things that don't matter.

People are prone to think of anger as a "bad emotion that must be fixed," but there are, of course, times when anger is a positive thing.

Animals also feel anger – like when they are faced with an enemy, and are trying to protect their lives. In times like these, feelings of anger emerge and the brain releases adrenaline. The body is preparing for war – it's the fight-or-flight response.

In fact, the original purpose of anger as an emotion is to promote the release of adrenaline in these tense situations. Without anger, animals become unable to protect themselves.

It's the same for us humans.

When people hear "anger management," they may assume it's a way of removing anger or irritation. However, this is not the case.

The goal of anger management is not to eradicate feelings of anger, but to create a balance between expressing the proper amount of anger when it's necessary, and keeping one's temper when it isn't.

There are both times when getting angry and not getting angry can cause regret. Regret from anger occurs when you wish you hadn't gotten angry about something. Regret from not getting angry happens when you think you should have gotten angry about something.

Reducing these feelings of regret is the goal of anger management.

I have personal experience with this. I got into a fight over something petty and alienated one of my friends. When I think back on it, there was absolutely no need to push a friend away over something as minor as this was.

There was also someone who often helped me out and would give me frank advice, but one time I got indignant about what they told me and I never contacted them again.

When I think about it now, the advice they gave me that day ending up having a big impact on making me who I am today. Yet, as much as I want to communicate my feelings of gratitude, I don't even know their contact information. No matter how much I regret how I acted, it's too late to do anything about it now.

Let's sum up. Anger management aims to provide the following:

1. Reduced feelings of regret due to anger

Anger management asserts that getting angry is not itself a problem. The goal is to move from "I got angry before I knew it" to "I chose to feel angry, and did."

"Choosing to feel angry" means taking responsibility for your anger. You can reduce a lot of your stress just by changing from "getting angry reflexively" to "getting angry by personal choice."

2. Proficiency at expressing anger

Anger, as an emotion, can be directed in 3 ways: towards people, towards oneself, and towards things (for more detail, see Part X Chapter X).

For example, if someone gets mad and says, "Why can't you do this?!" to someone else, that's anger directed towards people. If you attack yourself, wondering "Why am I such a loser?", that's anger directed towards oneself. If you slam doors or throw and break things, that's anger directed at objects.

By learning anger management, you can learn to express your anger without breaking things and without hurting others or yourself.

If you can communicate your anger well, nobody will be hurt or feel resentful if you get angry at them, and your relationships won't suffer.

What are the categories of "anger habits"?

Our anger intensity, aggressiveness, frequency, and duration are the traits that demand our scrutiny.

While I said that getting angry isn't bad in itself, if the way you get angry matches up with any of the following 4 criteria, there may be a problem. Do any seem to apply to you?

1. High intensity

"High intensity" refers to someone who goes from 0 to 100 when they get angry. Do you know anyone who gets so furious that people around them say, "Why are you getting so angry over this?"

2. Long duration

"Long duration" refers to holding grudges over very long periods of time, getting upset when remembering things, and being controlled by past anger.

3. High frequency

"High frequency" refers to frequently being in a state of irritation.

4. Aggressiveness

"Aggressiveness" refers to taking out one's anger on yourself, on people around you, or on things. Taking your anger out on people means attacking or blaming them. Taking your anger out on yourself means attacking or blaming yourself. Taking your anger out on things means breaking them or treating them badly.

Now let's try a self-diagnosis.

Take a look at the figure on the next page. The upper portion contains Intensity, Duration, and Frequency. The lower portion contains Aggressiveness (People, Self, Things).

Consider how each item relates to yourself and assign yourself a number of points.

How did you do? Did you get a sense of what tendencies your anger takes? Now imagine someone you know. Anyone is fine — friend, family, acquaintance, coworker, whoever.

Once you've made your selection, diagnose their anger for its Intensity, Duration, Frequency, and Aggressiveness. Give them scores on top of your own, using a different color or line type so you can differentiate them clearly.

What differences are there between yourself and the person you chose? What made you give them the score you did for Intensity? What was your basis for deciding Duration? Finally, what characteristics about this person led to your scores for Frequency and Aggressiveness?

We take in a lot of information when watching people. For example, when seeing someone we don't know yelling at shop staff, we tend to think they're the type of person that gets angry easily.

Conversely, the people around us are always taking in information about us without our realizing it.

If you don't want to be thought of as someone with "high anger intensity," you can learn to act in a way that will avoid that by understanding the nature of your intensity.

Similarly, if you don't want to be seen as the type of person who holds a grudge, it would be good to learn to act like someone who doesn't stay angry for a long time.

This is why it's so important to first understand your Anger Type and Characteristics (covered in chapters 2 and 3).

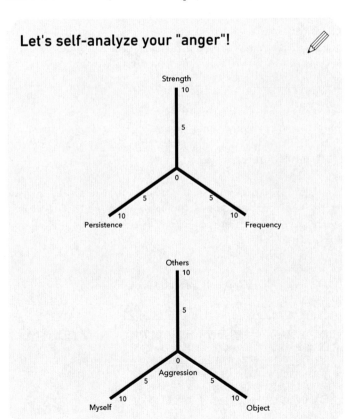

Let's self-analyze your "anger"!

Anger is a secondary emotion

Anger is something that arises from negative feelings such as frustration, sadness, or uncertainty.

So what are the mechanisms that cause anger?

In fact, anger doesn't exist on its own. Before feeling anger, there is always another emotion first.

Imagine that there is a cup inside your heart. Every day, we are pouring negative emotions – frustration, pain, loneliness, sadness, uncertainty – into this cup. These emotions are called primary emotions.

When the heart-cup becomes filled with negative primary emotions, the overflow comes out as "anger." Said another way, if the heart-cup doesn't contain a lot of primary emotions, not much anger will emerge either.

Have any of you experienced days where you're in a bad mood all day, from the second you wake up in the morning? That's because you're starting your morning with your cup full of negative emotions.

Anger is a secondary emotion

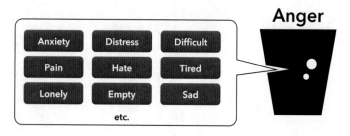

Usually, when people sleep they are able to clear some of their negativity, but if high-stress days pile up, they become unable to erase all their negative primary emotions in a single night.

When this happens, people are in a bad mood as soon as they wake up and are immediately irritated by the slightest thing.

It's no exaggeration to say that people get angry out of a desire to have these primary emotions to be recognized by others. By understanding this motivation behind anger, you can engage more effectively with people who are upset.

For example, consider the cliché of the disgruntled customer demanding to see someone in charge. At a store, this is usually a manager. At a company, it may be the president. At a school, it may be the principal.

People who press complaints like this have their heart-cups full of primary feelings like "I'm not being taken seriously," or "They're making a fool out of me." They instinctively know what it would take for them to feel like they are being taken seriously: if they can get access to someone with authority, they'll feel satisfied.

When you deal with someone who is angry, don't focus on their anger. Focus on the primary feeling that underlies it. Are they angry because they feel uneasy? Are they in pain? Are they in some kind of trouble?

It's common to say "I understand how you feel" to angry people. However, it's better to say this in reference not to their anger, but to the emotion they felt before their anger.

Of course, this isn't always enough to solve all problems. However, even if the issue isn't resolved, by showing someone that you understand their *primary* emotion, their trust and comfort with you should rise.

Incidentally, while there are people who tend to be angry and those who tend not to be angry, those who tend to be angry are ones with small heart-cups. Because their cup is small, their primary emotions overflow quickly.

This cup can be made bigger with training. This training is an excellent method for reducing your overall irritability levels (chapter 4 covers this in more detail).

Anger isn't something that arises instantaneously

Anger can be controlled via your interpretation of events.

There is a system as to how anger arises. If anger were something like an unfortunate accident that comes flying at you out of nowhere, leaving you defenseless, there would be nothing you could do about it.

However, that isn't the case. Just as there is a system to happiness, anger can also be controlled. People talk in Japan about getting angry "like an instant water boiler," but according to anger management, that can't actually happen.

People don't get angry instantaneously. Rather, anger always follows this 3-step pattern:

1. Recognition of an event

First, there must be an event to recognize. For example, perhaps you pointed out an error in an employee's work yesterday, but today they've made the same mistake in the same way.

2. Interpretation

Here, you interpret the event from 1 in some way. For example, you may think, "Yesterday I pointed out this mistake, so why are they making it again? Did they not understand me at all? They must be screwing around."

3. Becoming angry

Anger emerges based on the interpretation you applied in 2.

The most important step here is step 2: interpretation. You wouldn't get angry if instead you thought, "Did I not do a good job of explaining yesterday?" or "It looks like it would be good to point this out again today," or "Well, they're inexperienced, so this kind of mistake is understandable."

Having thoughts like this may instead lead you to think, "I'll train them a little more carefully," or, "It's cute of them to be making a mistake like this."

People can interpret the same events differently – even far enough as to find the same event enjoyable on one hand or irritating on the other.

Imagine that we all have a filter in front of our eyes. You can also imagine wearing a pair of glasses. If that filter or those glasses are clear, you will see things as they are.

However, if there is a tint to them, or if they are warped, you become unable to see straight. This disconnect with reality results in unpleasant feelings.

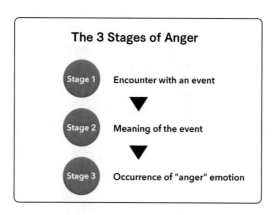

The 3 Stages of Anger

Stage 1   Encounter with an event

▼

Stage 2   Meaning of the event

▼

Stage 3   Occurrence of "anger" emotion

The true character of anger is "should"

We get angry when the "should" we believe in is violated before our eyes.

What is the true nature of the thing that warps our filter/glasses?

Imagine that an employee was told that he had to send an important e-mail to a client by 10AM. However, he forgot to send it. The same employee has made the same mistake before and he got in trouble for it.

Imagine you are his boss and you are upset about this. What specifically angers you, from the following categories?

1. Somebody

Maybe you are angry at the employee who made the mistake?

2. Event

Maybe you are angry that the e-mail wasn't sent in time? Alternatively, that the employee forgot to do an important task?

3. Associations based on 2

Maybe you are angry that in spite of this employee making this mistake in the past, now they've made it again? Or maybe you are disturbed at a sense that the employee thinks it's ok to make this kind of mistake?

All of them seem like things you might get mad about, but it's actually fairly hard to put your finger on it exactly, isn't it?

If you think it's the employee, that seems like it could be right. But if you think it's the event, that seems right too. It also might seem like a combination.

They all seem like things to be angry about, but actually picking one is difficult.

That's because, strictly speaking, it's none of these.

In fact, we aren't angry with somebody, and we're not angry about some event. We're also not angry about the associations with it.

The true character of our anger lies in the word "should." That is, "This should be done," "This should not be done."

What makes us angry is seeing the "should" we believe in violated in front of us. In this case, it's "He should send mails on time," or maybe, "He should take instructions seriously." Seeing these beliefs violated infuriates us.

If you understand what kind of "shoulds" you believe in, you can get a sense of when and in what situations you are likely to get angry.

Try imagining a time when you got angry recently. Behind that anger, you will find a "should" hidden. Try clarifying what that "should" is.

For example, let's say your train comes late in the morning and you feel irritated. Behind that, you may be thinking, "Trains should arrive right on time."

Or, let's say someone bumps into you on the street while looking at their smartphone and you get upset. In your heart, you're thinking something like, "People shouldn't walk while using their smartphones."

What do you think? Do you find it easier to find reasons for your anger by using "should"?

In fact, this "should" is exactly what warps your filter or glasses mentioned earlier.

It's hard dealing with "should"

By training your emotions, you can broaden the range of your "shoulds."

By getting better at using "should," anger management gets easier. However, keep in mind that the following three things makes dealing with "should" more difficult.

1. Believing that one's own "should" is always right

All the "shoulds" a person believes in are right — at least, to the person who believes in them.

That applies even for "shoulds" about problems in society made at a glance — or even without that much. It doesn't matter — to the person who believes it, it has to be right.

2. "Should" is a matter of degree

Many "shoulds" are a matter of degree. For example, people say, "People should be on time." Some people consider being 5 minutes early necessary for being on time. Other people think arriving right on time is fine.

Even though both of these people have the same "should" idea about being on time, in reality, the degree between them varies.

3. "Should" changes with time and location

"Should" is something that changes with time and location.

For example, 30 years ago, children were taught to say hello to people they see — including strangers. Now, if anything, it's the opposite. In order to keep children safe, they are taught not to talk to people they don't know. Similarly, children are all taught that they should not lie, but as they get older, they encounter the idea that circumstances may justify deception.

In this way, "should" is something that can depend on context. But what can be done to deal with "should" effectively? There is an effective method. The basic approach is described in detail in the training discussed in chapter 4.

I hope everyone now understands the mechanisms behind the emotion of anger.

I have explained how, in order to become proficient at handling anger, you must first know your individual emotional habits and "anger type." In the chapter that follows, I will discuss personality traits, anger habits, and training methods for improvement unique to each anger type.

Chapter 2

Know Your Anger Habits

You can learn your anger type with an anger management diagnostic test!

The anger management diagnostic test parses your experience of anger. It clarifies what kinds of situations make you liable to feel anger and what your triggers are.

I discussed this in chapter 1 also, but I want to reiterate that anger is a very natural emotion. It is something necessary for human beings. Anger is not bad in itself.

However, it is important to be able to tell the difference between things worth and not worth causing you anger. If you become able to identify things that don't require an angry response, you will become able to prevent issues in your interpersonal relationships.

For example, have you ever given in to emotion and gotten angry at somebody working under you, only to regret it later when you realized it wasn't necessary? If you get angry in a way that you later regret, that may be a sign that you didn't need to get angry at all.

In contrast, there are also times when you should have gotten mad but didn't.

By taking the anger management diagnostic test, you can understand your own anger tendencies and characteristics and learn to not give in to your emotions.

Please note: there is no "good" or "bad" to the test result. It is merely an impression of your current state of mind.

Your "Anger Type"
(Simple Anger Management Diagnostic Test)

STEP 1

For each of the questions below, choose the answer that is closest to how you feel:

Strongly disagree	(1 point)
Disagree	(2 points)
Slightly disagree	(3 points)
Slightly agree	(4 points)
Agree	(5 points)
Strongly agree	(6 points)

Then assign yourself points based on the answer you chose.

☐	Q01	The world has rules that should be respected, and people should follow them
☐	Q02	I want to investigate things until I feel satisfied
☐	Q03	I believe that what I'm doing is right
☐	Q04	I often misunderstand people's feelings
☐	Q05	I think people are more evil than good by nature
☐	Q06	People should state clearly what they want to say
☐	Q07	Not even small mistakes should escape unnoticed
☐	Q08	I have strong likes and dislikes
☐	Q09	I worry about what the people around me say about me
☐	Q10	I follow rules I make myself
☐	Q11	I'm not good at taking in what other people say
☐	Q12	I tend to act without thinking

STEP 2

Once you have assigned points to each question,
add them up in the following way:

☐	1. Q1 + Q7
☐	2. Q2 + Q8
☐	3. Q3 + Q9
☐	4. Q4 + Q10
☐	5. Q5 + Q11
☐	6. Q6 + Q12

Which one has the highest score? ☐

*   If you have ties in 2 or more categories,
    assign yourself all of the tie categories.

Results are on the next page!

Results

1. You are the **JUST AND UPRIGHT** type	(page 41)
2. You are the **LEARNED AND TALENTED** type	(page 49)
3. You are the **POMP AND CIRCUMSTANCE** type	(page 57)
4. You are the **GENTLE BUT FIRM** type	(page 65)
5. You are the **CAREFUL AND VIGILANT** type	(page 73)
6. You are the **NAIVE AND INNOCENT** type	(page 81)

*   If you have ties in 2 or more categories,
    you may be a combination of those types.

Now let's take a look at each of the anger types and their path to improvement.

TYPE 1

JUST AND UPRIGHT

The defender of justice charges in!

You have a strong sense of justice and conviction, and do not hesitate to act on those feelings. You get fired up by having a sense of purpose, and charge straight ahead without wavering in your beliefs.

1 | Type Characteristics

Strong Points

Making a ruckus on the train without considering the people around you is inexcusable.

That's the Just and Upright type in a nutshell. They have the courage to confront impolite people directly. Their sense of justice is strong and they possess lofty ethical ideas. They keep the order of things and diligently enforce what is good and proper. They are true to their beliefs and act on them directly. In addition, because they have strong wills, they are not easily swayed. They have follow-through, yet also have a side that can think about things calmly.

Weak Points

People who have a strong sense of justice tend to be seen as hard-to-please by the people around them. Their strong sense of duty can cause them to take on more work than they can actually handle. Because of their diligence and ambition, they tend to be hard on themselves. They are hard on the people around them too, and have a tendency to push their ideas about society's rules and manners on others.

It is important to be right, but it's good to consider time and place as well.

2 | Anger Habits

With your strong sense of justice and unbendable beliefs, you have a tendency to interfere more than necessary when you think others are doing something wrong.

- Even when you don't have the authority to judge, you can't help but feel you have to do it.
- You think that in order to serve justice, sometimes it's necessary to overstep your boundaries.
- You strongly feel that you need to provide discipline.
- You can't overlook things that aren't right — even if it's just a little.

3 | Keywords Behind the Anger

When you feel anger, certain keywords are often hidden behind it. For example, when you get annoyed seeing someone on the train violating train manners, or finding out about a celebrity's adultery on TV, the words "manners" and "morality" are often somewhere nearby.

Morality	Justice	Ethics	Judgment
Manners	Discipline	Parenting	

4 | Improvement Training

Unless we are in a particular profession, like judge or policeman, we don't have the authority to judge or punish others. We cannot dole out vigilante justice. We are free to offer our critiques of others, but that is not the same as punishment.

Try thinking about the things that make you angry in terms of what you can/cannot do and what is/is not important. It's fine to do the things you can do, but strive to accept the things you cannot do and draw a line there.

Training for what you can and can't do

Even if something angers us, there are things we can and can't do.

What can we do? What can't we do? When we are led astray by our anger, often we lose sight of where the line between these lies.

For example, let's say you see someone misbehaving on the train. Is changing them something you can do, or can't?

Let's say you feel anger at a TV celebrity's private misconduct and want to do something about it. Is changing that celebrity something you can do, or something you can't?

You are free to act on your anger, but if you give into it, you could get yourself into trouble or expose yourself to unhealthy levels of stress.

Things you can do:
Example Give the person misbehaving on the train a warning.

Things you can't do:
Example Make a cheating celebrity stop their affair.

5 | How to Identify this Type

Because this type of person has faith in their own sense of justice and ethics, they tend to harshly criticize others for the smallest deviance. They are able to forgive people who can offer a good justification for their behavior, but are prone to thinking of people who repeat their misdeeds as evil.

6 | How to Interact with this Type

(Boss)

Let's say your boss says something that seems inappropriate, like, "I'm your supervisor, so you need to inform me about what happens to you over weekends." When they say this, they believe it is right to do so.

For things that are outside of your job expectations, it is best to firmly tell your boss that those things are outside of your job expectations. This kind of boss has no ill intent. They are trying to guide their employees down the right path, like a parent. They are, in fact, very reliable people.

(Employee)

Even when talking to a supervisor, if this type of employee sees something they think is wrong, they will point it out. They think that if their argument is sound, anything they say will be forgiven.

Because this type is driven by their sense of duty, explain to them your high expectations for them. They may think that what they are saying is right, but occasionally it isn't. Try to carefully explain to them what is correct and incorrect in terms of facts.

(Friend)

As a friend, this type will sometimes say things with a patronizing tone and make you self-conscious.

This may be annoying, but understand that they say it out of concern for you. Just saying "OK" or "Thanks" is enough to make them happy. They are not good at overlooking crookedness, but they are also very loyal and can make good friends.

(Partner/Lover)

Everyday life can be challenging with someone who can't accept the flaws of another. If not addressed, this lack of acceptance can develop into mobbing behavior or domestic violence.

The Just and Upright type is rigid about their beliefs, so opposing them directly won't be successful. Instead, try to frame opinions and demands that they dislike in terms of discussions and requests.

7 | Suitable Industries and Professions

The Just and Upright character can express itself most freely in positions related to protecting society, such as legal professions like law and the judiciary and law enforcement professions like the police, prosecution, or auditing.

Type 2

LEARNED AND TALENTED

This fastidious perfectionist gets everything done right!

This type has a tendency to see things in black and white. They think in terms of extremes with their likes and dislikes, enemies and friends, good and evil, etc. They are perfectionists and often can't get anything started or finished unless they feel they can meet their own standards.

While their likes and dislikes are highly defined, they tend to maintain a degree of distance and moderation in their relations.

1 | Type Characteristics

Strong Points

This type is always making rational, logical, clear-headed judgments. They are sensitive, polite perfectionists always in pursuit of their best self. They try their hardest even in difficult environments and have the power to accomplish things. They are ambitious and are able to proactively advance themselves by always studying and learning.

Weak points

This type cannot tolerate indecisiveness. They do not deal well with people who lack powers of discernment or take ambiguous positions. They also tend to see everything in terms of black and white. As a result, they are unable to remain neutral, and come to extreme conclusions about whether something is good or bad or whether or not they like something.

Since this type easily feels stressed around people who don't share their values, they may try to avoid discomfort by only spending time with people who agree with them, which can lead to a narrowing of their network.

2 | Anger Habits

There is more that is gray in the world than black or white. This type is often frustrated by the large number of things that exist without clear distinction.

Because they have no patience for indecisive people, they don't get along well with those who take a while to reach a judgment or think in vague, equivocal terms.

- No patience for indecision or people who can't clearly state their likes and dislikes
- Inability to start or finish things due to excessive perfectionism
- Tendency to exclude people who don't agree with them
- Not good at showing tolerance

3 | Keywords Behind the Anger

When you feel anger, the following keywords are often hidden behind it. For example, when you feel frustrated when someone acts in a wishy-washy way, the words "dualism" and "perfectionist" are often somewhere nearby.

Dualism	Exclusionary	Perfectionist
Meticulousness	Anti-Neutrality	Intolerance

4 | Improvement Training

There are multiple sides to everything – few things can be rendered in terms of black and white. If you try to interpret everything as a binary, the things you can accept dwindle, and your tolerance dwindles as well.

Try to consider alternative viewpoints before splitting things in two. Ask yourself, "Can it be seen from another angle?" "What might someone else think of this?"

"Three Sides" Training

Everything has three sides: a subjective side, an objective side, and a factual side. The goal of this exercise is to separate out each of these things, and then write them down.

For example, let's say that you encounter your close friend, A, having a friendly conversation with B, who often speaks poorly about you. You may think to yourself, "Why is A, who is supposed to be my friend, with that B guy?! A must be saying bad things about me too!" This is your subjective interpretation of the event.

In contrast, the "objective" interpretation is simply, "My friend A is talking to B about something." Then, let's say that in this case, the "factual" side of what happened is that A and B simply ran into each other unexpectedly and were having a conversation about work.

Obviously, focusing on just the "subjective" interpretation emphasizes your personal interpretation. Looking at it objectively, however, you become able to see things from another perspective.

There are times when you can't know the facts, but there is still only one set of facts. By splitting things up in this fashion, you can learn to avoid seeing things in absolutes.

Subjective

Example A and B were together. They must have been saying bad things about me.

Objective

Example A and B were talking about something.

Factual

Example A and B happened to meet and were talking about work.

5 | How to Identify this Type

This type will state their preferences clearly and judge things as good or bad.
Once they come to a determination they are quick to act – but because they seek perfection in their work, they have a hard time starting things or ending things unless they feel satisfied.

6 | How to Deal with this Type

(Boss)

This type of boss hates vague reports. They demand clearly stated opinions on the good and the bad, the merits and the demerits, on everything. The reality is that there are often gray zones. Nonetheless, try to offer clearly stated opinions on which plan of action you think is better.

To the extent that final decisions require their approval, things will go more smoothly if you prepare objective data in advance.

(Employee)

An employee of this type will be irritated if you are indecisive, so make decisions quickly and give explicit instructions on how you want things done. This type prefers a supervisor that exerts strong leadership to one that discusses matters with employees.

(Friend)

Even if you think you're friends with someone of this type, they may not think the same of you. They can have very particular criteria for what people are placed in that category.

If you notice a discrepancy between how you and other friends are treated, you may have been placed into their "incompetent person" category. If you try to force the distance between the two of you to close, you may just make it larger.

(Partners and Lovers)

This type has no tolerance for indecisiveness or loose behavior, so care must be taken when living with them. If you let your guard down or get too casual too fast after getting close, they may change their mind about you in an instant.

7 | Suitable Industries and Professions

The Learned and Talented type does best in a role that lets them express their perfectionist, methodical personality. They do well as researchers, engineers, manufacturers, etc.

Their persistence and attention to detail also makes them good as editors and designers.

Type 3

POMP AND CIRCUMSTANCE

This immaculate leader will put their trust in you!

This type has a lot of pride and possesses a gorgeous, elegant aura. They tend to be attracted to jobs that offer them status and recognition.
They are proficient at self-evaluation and have the confidence to move ever forward.
They have a very "leader-like" presence.

1 | Type Characteristics

Strengths

This type never buckles under pressure and always maintains a dignified air. They are proactive and look after others well. Because of the sense of victory they exude, they naturally tend to be seen as leaders by others – and they strive to live up to those expectations.

Weaknesses

This type has a tendency to be overconfident and narcissistic. They don't feel any sense of guilt about controlling others, and sometimes will try to coerce the people around them in a heavy-handed manner. They also tend to respond poorly to criticism, and can only open up to people who understand them. It may seem as though they can get along with anyone, but often these relationships are quite superficial.

2 | Anger Habits

Because of their pride, they can get angry if they are treated badly or as though they are unimportant. While they are capable of self-critique, they are also very sensitive to critique from others.

- Can be overconfident and narcissistic
- Can become arrogant from their large amounts of pride
- Believe themselves to be chosen individuals
- They strongly want to feel needed by others
- They tend to confuse rights, duties, and desires

3 | Keywords Behind the Anger

When you feel anger, the following keywords are often hidden behind it. For example, when you get upset because you think someone has criticized you or you aren't being treated properly, the words "conceit" and "pride" are often lurking beneath.

Conceit	Presumption	"Need for control"
Pride	"Might makes right"	Me
Arrogance		

4 | Improvement training

If you get upset at someone — saying, "Why won't you do what I tell you?!" — ask yourself if your frustration arises from your "right," your "duty," or your "desire."

"Duty" is something that *must* be done. "Desire" is just a personal want. "Right" refers to the ability or privilege to do or receive something.

If you become able to identify which of these apply when you want somebody to do something, you can learn to avoid getting upset about trivial things.

Learning to distinguish between "duties," "rights," and "desires."

When you get angry, try to analyze what happened in terms of "rights," "duties," and "desires."

For example, let's say that you are at work, working overtime. Even though there's so much work that you are staying late, your employee is trying to go home.

When you see this, you might think, "What is that guy thinking, going home when their boss is still here, working so hard?" However, this demonstrates a conflation of "rights," "duties," and "desires."

Right

Example If an employee finishes their work early, they can go home early.

Duty

Example Employees must do the work they are assigned in accordance with their role.

Desire

Example If an employee is finished with their work, you want them to help you.

Wanting an employee to help you before they go home is your "desire." As a supervisor, you are thinking about the employee in terms of their "duty," but the employee has the "right" to go home early. By not giving in to anger and by not confusing "rights," "duties," and "desires," you can avoid getting upset by what your employee is doing.

5 | How to Identify this Type

This type always has a "victor's aura" about them. Regardless of if they have the objective results and abilities to back it up, their high amounts of self-respect create this sensation. That said, because they want recognition from others, they will often go around asking what people think of them.

6 | How to Interact with this Type

(Boss)

This type makes for dependable supervisors because of their strong leadership, but they tend to be hard on their employees. In order to avoid rousing their anger, it is wise to observe their behavioral pattern and try to stay one step ahead of them.

They have a tendency to not value employees who are slow to act or make decisions. However, they often think that if they themselves are doing overtime, employees should be doing overtime as well.

If they make unreasonable demands, avoid confronting them head on. Try offering an excuse of some kind, like, "I'm not feeling well, so I'm going to head home now."

(Employee)

This type of employee can get very upset if you hurt their pride. For example, if you call them by the wrong name, they may loudly correct you. Even small things like this can demotivate them.

They can be difficult, but try adopting an attitude that shows that you care about them. They are the type that can release their full potential by having their confidence boosted like this.

(Friend)

People with a lot of pride think their opinion is more important than anything. If someone contradicts them or points out a mistake they made, they can become instantly upset.

Just humor them and agree with what they say. If there is something you want to disagree with, it is effective to first acknowledge their ideas, saying, "Yes, that may be right," and then stating your opinion.

(Partners and Lovers)

As a leader through-and-through, they want to feel needed by everyone. Don't be afraid to show your weak side and ask for help – it works. This type often feels better when flattered like this.

This type has a tendency to be aggressive in making demands, and often thinks, "I do all of these things for people, so it's natural for others to do the same for me." Consequently, be sure to always show gratitude to them for their help.

7 | Suitable Industries and Professions

This type does well in professions for which interacting with others is a major element, like advertisement and management. They are gregarious with people they meet for the first time, can make quick judgments if trouble arises, and can take action.

They are also suited to consultancy or director-like positions.

Type 4

GENTLE BUT FIRM

A charming contrast?
The warrior with singular purpose

*This type has a gentle, mild aura to them,
but has great strength hidden inside. Because of the
contrast between their exterior and interior,
they are often misunderstood by people.
They have their own personal code,
and can be identified by their efforts to get others to
agree with them or conform to their model.*

1 | Type Characteristics

Strengths

The GENTLE BUT FIRM type, as the name suggests, has an iron will wrapped in a pleasant appearance. That will comes from a conviction that the things that they think and decide upon are important. They have a sense of responsibility and independence, making them reliable people no matter where they are.

Weaknesses

This type's weakness arises from the things on which they refuse to compromise. They also can end up with convictions with little basis in reality.

When this happens, they are not very good at listening to what others have to say about it, and end up in a vicious cycle where they continue to believe whatever they want.

2 | Anger Habits

Because this type often seems calm on the surface, they are often taken advantage of by others, which leads to stress.

Because they believe in the code and rules they have created for themselves, if they reluctantly try to do something that displeases them, they can feel extreme frustration.

- Unable to change their way of thinking
- No tolerance for things that don't conform to their rules
- Suspicious of other people's feelings
- Tend to think that everyone should think the same way as them, without justification

- Persist in their beliefs even without evidence
- Not good at listening to others
- Not good at organization

3 | Keywords Behind the Anger

When you feel anger, the following keywords are often hidden behind it. For example, when you are upset when something is different from how you thought it was or things aren't going along with the procedure you decided on, the words "code" and "assumption" are often behind it.

Stubborn	Assumption	Mind-reading
Code	Inflexible	

4 | Improvement Training

If you think things like, "everyone is this way," "it's common sense," or "they're the ones who are wrong," you may be thinking in terms of your own code.

Try to always check whether or not your expectation is just your own idea about things.

Moreover, remind yourself that other people have their own perspectives, and just as you have things that are important to you, others have things that are important to them.

If you start to feel suspicious, try to keep your focus on the good things about other people and things.

Learning to differentiate "assumptions" and "facts"

All of us have a tendency to confuse our "assumptions" with "facts." If you have big assumptions, reality will start to look warped.

Hypothetically speaking, even if your assumptions are disconnected from reality, all you need to do is proactively seek the truth. However, many people assume that the truth will be a difficult and inconvenient thing for them to accept.

Assumption

Example The only way to get to X City is by plane.

Fact

Example Actually, in order to get to X City, one can take a plane or an overnight bus.

For example, let's pretend that you believe that Method A is the only way to get some kind of work done. However, believing that Method A is the only possible method may be an *assumption*. In reality, it turns out that there is also Method B and Method C *(fact)*. It may even be possible to reach some goal more easily that way.

By learning to separate *facts* and *assumptions* in this way, you can become able to assess things in a neutral fashion.

5 | How to Identify this Type

This type is usually mild-mannered, but once their anger fuse is lit, the intensity of their assumptions and distorted thinking comes to the surface, creating a startling contrast with their typical behavior.

Because of their strong insistence on their individuality, they may appear to be listening to what their friends are saying, but just ignore it and contribute silently.

6 | How to Interact with this Type

(Boss)

Because this type cherishes having their own pace and way of doing things, try to avoid getting in their way. Once they get upset, they lose all flexibility and it is difficult to get them to listen to the opinion of someone below them.

When that happens, let some time pass and look for the right timing to approach them with a request.

(Employee)

This type is stubborn about how they do things and can become quite narrow-minded. If you tell them to think more broadly, they may not be able to push themselves to do it even if at heart they agree with you.

Instead of dropping big new ideas on them all at once, try guiding them towards a new place one small step at a time.

Because they are resistant to big changes in method, come up with a scheme that changes only one thing at a time.

(Friend)

The longer you know this type and become closer to them, the more they tend to believe that you hold the same beliefs as them.

When dealing with people with their own code, avoid pointing out their misunderstandings. Instead, first point out what is right about their ideas. This will allow for a calm conversation.

(Partners and Lovers)

When this type has ideas pushed on them or is criticized or attacked, they tend to retaliate in a tit-for-tat way.

In order to avoid a fight, first quell your own desire to escalate and begin by saying, "Yes, you may be right," acknowledging their ideas.

7 | Suitable Industries and Professions

Because of their adherence to their own idiosyncratic ruleset, jobs where individuality is important – like in styling, baking, or cooking – or jobs that involve dedication to one thing – like being an artisan or programmer – are ideal.

Type 5

CAREFUL AND VIGILANT

The strategist who never fights a losing battle

This type is watchful and prudent, able to avoid conflict with those around them. However, the fact that they get along equally well with everyone means, by the same token, that they aren't particularly close to anyone.

They are smart and tend to overthink interpersonal relationships and can be superficial in their efforts to please everyone.

1 | Type Characteristics

Strengths

People of this type think fast and are good judges of character, making them tacticians able to unravel complicated relationships. They get the sense of things quickly and are able to deal with everyone tactfully.

They are always cautious and think carefully before acting, never fighting battles they can't win. For that reason, they give peace of mind to their supervisors.

Weaknesses

Behind their sensible, civil exterior is a suspicious heart that does not open easily, with a timidity that makes them slow to trust others.

They do not have high opinions of themselves and tend to be oversensitive to criticism, which means that they can have a hard time taking action.

2 | Anger Habits

This type doesn't open up easily, but has a tendency to label people. "This person is X." "That person is Y." As a result, their relationships can fail to go smoothly and their stress builds.

They also tend to be excessively pessimistic. They use extreme language, like "Nobody values me," and can see themselves as the main character of a tragedy.

- Unable to trust others
- Cautious to the point of inaction
- Tendency to label others
- Can suffer from an inferiority complex
- Builds walls between themselves and others, making healthy relationships difficult to make

3 | Keywords Behind the Anger

When this type feels angry, certain keywords are often lurking beneath. For example, if you get upset after seeing someone doing better than you or if someone acts too familiar with you, the keywords "inferiority complex" and "jealousy" are hiding behind your emotion.

Jealousy	Suspicion	Pessimism	Inferiority
Labelling	Prejudice	Envy	

4 | Improvement Training

When you label someone, this is proof that you aren't watching them closely. In order to create healthy human relationships, you must try to observe them carefully. It is also important to open your heart and let others know what kind of person you are.

This type uses exaggerated language in an effort to justify themselves. However, if this is repeated, they can start to think of themselves as the main character in a tragedy, even if the situation doesn't warrant it.

In order to avoid twisting the facts, try to avoid exaggerated language and state things as they are.

Finding exceptions to break the vicious cycle

This type has a tendency to interpret their inferiority complex as jealousy, to be envious of others, and to think of their lives as tragic.

In order to break this pattern, try to look back on past events and look for exceptions. Try answering the following questions.

1. In what situations did trying something
   different go well?

2. What did you do in those situations?

3. When did you do this?

4. Where did you do this?

5. Were you with anyone at the time?

Let's find the "exceptions" and break the vicious cycle!

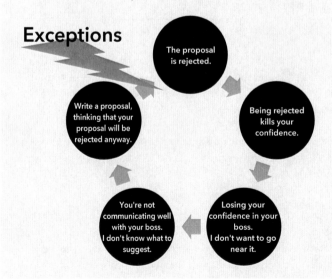

Exceptions

The proposal is rejected.

Being rejected kills your confidence.

Losing your confidence in your boss. I don't want to go near it.

You're not communicating well with your boss. I don't know what to suggest.

Write a proposal, thinking that your proposal will be rejected anyway.

5 | How to identify this type

At a glance, this type seems very social. Out of an extreme desire to avoid being hated by others, they have an excessive amount of concern for what others think of them.

Because of their vigilant nature, there is no one they would call a close friend no matter how large their social circle. Because they prioritize keeping distance from others, they inquire after others as little as possible, and hate it when others pry into their own affairs. They are serious about maintaining their personal space.

It's common for this type to use extreme language like "it's the worst" or "it's pointless now." They tend not to use positive language and are excessively negative.

6 | How to Interact with this Type

(Boss)

Even if it seems like a boss of this type is listening to you, they may not actually be engaged. Sometimes they may privately be feeling angry or resentful.

Be careful not to look down on or be contemptuous of your boss if they don't criticize or object. Be sure to keep their position in mind.

(Employee)

Because this type often feels undervalued, they tend to hesitate to promote their own ideas. In order to hear what this employee really thinks, you need to create an environment in which they feel safe.

It's best to approach this type with the recognition that they don't open up easily and that it will take a while to create a relationship with them.

(Friend)

This type doesn't want to be hated, so they tend to go along with whatever others say. Don't be hasty and assume you get along with this person well – you're misinterpreting their reaction. They are just humoring you.

(Partners and Lovers)

Because this type is always polite and kind, it may sometimes seem like they are interested in someone or other. However, understand that they are just doing this to avoid being disliked.

Because it takes a long time for this type to open up, it takes a while to create a relationship – even if you have nothing but good will towards them.

7 | Suitable Industries and Professions

Because this type has a serious, watchful character, professions that involve money and the manipulation of numbers – like finance, economics, and accounting – are a good fit.

On the other hand, workplaces with complex human relationships are exhausting. Environments with more sterile social exchanges are ideal.

Type 6

NAIVE AND INNOCENT

The free spirit who wants everything to go their way

This type blurts out whatever they're thinking and acts on it. Because they can express themselves so directly, they excel at bringing things together. They make for good leaders.

1 | Type Characteristics

Strengths

This type sees the possibilities in everything and has the strength to see things through to success. They are good at talking and are able to express their unfiltered opinion, whether before a crowd or one-on-one.

This type loves debate, and they believe that by arguing with someone with a different opinion, both people can deepen their understanding and grow from it.

Weaknesses

Because this is a "just do it" type of person, they aren't good at considering the feelings of others. They are assertive and can overreach or become tyrannical.

They yearn for power and authority and can feel very frustrated when they think their views aren't getting through. They have the ability to lead an organization, but they can occasionally be too heavy-handed. They should be careful not to act rashly.

2 | Anger Habits

Because this type is forceful in their assertiveness, they can feel great stress and frustration if they find themselves in a position where they can't speak their mind or be understood.

If that dissatisfaction is not resolved, they can lose sight of consequences and aggressively try to persuade people who disagree or try to intimidate them by yelling, which can lead to trouble.

- Always need to have their opinion heard
- Critical and antagonistic towards others
- Believe that pressuring or stating things more resolutely can get others to change
- Believe that others must feel the same way as them

3 | Keywords Behind the Anger

When this type feels angry, certain keywords are often hidden behind the anger. For example, if you get upset because you can't act on your curiosity or because someone won't change their mind after telling them something, the terms "assertion" and "self-righteous" are lurking beneath.

Assertion	Self-righteous	Oppressive
Critical	Independent	Authoritarian

4 | Improvement Training

People cannot be changed by force. They do not change because someone pressures them, but because they decide for themselves that they want to change.

Even if it was possible to change them by force, this method doesn't create healthy, long-lasting relationships. Somebody not changing isn't a sign that they are bad or that you are bad.

"Different strokes for different folks." "There's no accounting for taste." Just as these phrases suggest, people's values and preferences are different. It is only natural that there are people who will be different from you.

When you meet someone who is different from you, be curious. Challenge yourself to discover if you can think the same way they do.

"Supporting role" training

This type always wants to be the lead role, and isn't very good at considering the feelings of others. What would the person you're talking to think if you tried to push 100% of your ideas onto them?

When I try to get a subordinate to do a job that I believe makes sense to me (example)

	Myself	Employee
100%	No talking back, no questions. That's what I expect.	I may be told afterwards that I forced them to do something, or they may do it unwillingly.
70%	Some questions are allowed about what to do. However, not doing it is not an option. Is this the most control I can let them have?	I think they'll do it even if they have some doubts, but they may not be that productive.
50%	Some choice is allowed, and it's ok to say whether or not there's a point to doing something and if they want to do it. If they make a big deal about it, maybe it doesn't need to be done.	I think that if they decide on their own to do it, they'll work as hard as they can.
30%	I don't offer my own opinion. I leave it all to them. If it's like this, maybe there's no real reason to do it at all.	They probably won't do it.

Try running these simulations at 70%, 50%, etc. In this way, you can get a sense of how other people might feel and act in a more tolerant way with them.

5 | How to Identify this Type

This type wants to be respected, praised, and recognized by society. They love being the center of attention. They have a lively aura and talk loudly with big gestures in a way that makes their presence known.

For better or for worse, this type isn't great at reading social cues. They can't keep quiet about what they want to say and can freeze a room by blurting out whatever is on their mind.

6 | How to Interact with this Type

(Boss)

This type can be oppressive, but they mean no harm. Rather, they may be trying their hardest, which results in them acting in tyrannical ways.

Because they can be capricious, they often make changes to their course of action. They don't see anything wrong with this.

However, there should be a pattern to the things this type of boss looks into seriously and the kinds of things they say off-the-cuff. As an employee, it would be wise to learn the difference between them.

Because they are good at looking after others, you can count on them to help you if you rely on them. Feel free to do so more.

(Employee)

Because this type acts before thinking, they are quite proactive. However, they can be impertinent and slow with Ho-Ren-So.

(Japanese business term for "report, communicate, discuss")

This type is able to get things done, but there's not much that can be done to smooth them out. If you anticipate what they'll do and create plans based on that, they can make the most of their abilities.

(Friend)

This type tends to move at their own pace and are moodmakers of a sort. They tend to stir things up because they like to stick their nose in everything, but they bear no malice. Think of them as perpetual children and watch over them warmly.

(Partners and Lovers)

This type can behave arrogantly. Sometimes they can try to settle things forcefully in arguments. Once they start talking, they want to be able to do as they please until they calm down.

If you fight fire with fire, the situation will only get worse. If you can learn to redirect their force, like in aikidō, you can avoid pointless arguments.

7 | Suitable Industries and Professions

This type excels in work that lets them express their curiosity and vitality, such as in entrepreneurship or handling project planning in development departments.

Because they get frustrated if they can't do the things they like, they need a workplace that lets them do independent, creative work. For better or for worse, they aren't meek people. They do well in positions that don't seem to suit them.

Chapter 3

Differentiating Anger Tendencies
Learn to Control Your Anger
Habits

By understanding the characteristics of your anger, you can learn to deal with your angry feelings. In so doing, your relationships with your supervisors, colleagues, employees working for you, clients, customers, and your family will improve.

This chapter looks at the traits of people who exhibit high intensity, duration, frequency, or aggressiveness in their anger. It then discusses ways to improve in the areas that apply to you.

1 | Anger Intensity

Try to evaluate the intensity of your anger using the 10 point scale below.

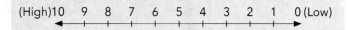

(High)10 9 8 7 6 5 4 3 2 1 0 (Low)

"Intensity" refers to the strength of your anger.

People's reactions to the same unpleasant event are different. There are people who explode over the smallest thing, people who take the same thing in stride, and people who quietly seethe about it but don't show it.

People with high anger intensity tend to get far more angry than necessary once their fuse has been lit. Even if the other party apologizes, the anger continues until it all gets exhausted. This sort of excessive anger is like dry tinder under your life. It constantly threatens to set fire to your health, your relationships, your career, and your parenting.

Once this is realized, people with intense anger may think they have nothing but flaws. However, this isn't the case at all.

People with intense anger – in other words, people who act on their emotions – are people who are able to express themselves naturally. For that reason, equating "strong anger" with "bad" and trying to put a lid on yourself isn't the right thing to do. Instead, aim to control it.

People with low intensity anger tend not to get very angry even when they are, in fact, angry. Certainly, these people have a gentle and sensitive character. However, not getting angry because you have *chosen* pacifism is one thing. Not getting angry because you don't have the willpower or courage to get angry is something else.

Sometimes, people don't seem to have high anger intensity because they are constantly pushing their anger inside themselves. Caution is needed if this is the case.

People with intense anger are:
- Assertive
- Rough in their behavior
- High-handed

A prescription for your anger

People with intense anger want to express their anger once they feel it, which leads to them getting angrier than necessary. An effective method to deal with this is to think calmly about how angry you are whenever you feel upset.

Method 1 Take your temperature

People say that they start to feel hot from their anger. Let's try recording it.

Measure your "temperature" on a 10-point scale. 0 means being totally at peace, while 10 is the angriest you've ever felt in your life. From now on, try thinking of how strong your anger is when you feel it.

In the beginning, you may start comparing the scores. "If I give a 4 to this, the 2 I gave last time doesn't make sense," or "If that thing last time was a 2, it doesn't seem right to give a 5 here."

Once you get into the habit of doing this, you will get a better understanding of how angry you are in a relative sense, and you

Let's record our anger on a scale of 10.

Strong

10 — "Absolutely unforgivable!!! The biggest rage of my life.

9
8 — I feel resentment. Pretty strong anger.
7

6
5 — A little strong anger that lingers even whilst trying to stay calm.
4

3
2 — Just a little bit of anger which can be acknowledged.
1

0 — No anger. Calm.

Weak

will start to learn not to get angrier than necessary.

Method 2 Increase your Anger Vocabulary

"Irritated," "pissed," "upset," "furious," "annoyed," "losing one's temper," "trembling with rage," "wrathful." There are lots of ways in English to express your anger.

People who can only think of "annoyed," "mad," and "pissed" when expressing themselves to others have limited themselves to 3 categories – but anger, as an emotion, covers a wide range of feelings.

If you've only got 3 words to use, you might say you're pissed or mad even when you're just a little annoyed.

If you have intense anger, try to increase your vocabulary for describing your anger. When anger bubbles up from within, try to think about what word best describes your feelings in the moment.

If you become familiar with 5 words, you can express 5 levels of anger. If you become familiar with 10 words, you can communicate 10 levels.

There's a huge number of words for describing anger. That's because "anger" is a very broad emotion.

How to interact with people with intense anger

If people with intense anger are in your life, what should you do about them? Just being around explosive anger can be intimidating and wear you out.

First, try observing the anger of these people while keeping the following 3 points in mind.

Point 1 Understand Patterns

There are defined patterns to the timing, place, and people involved when someone gets angry.

For example, they may always be irritated in the hectic moments before heading out to work in the morning, or start to feel agitated in high-stress environments such as hospitals or crowded subways, or depressed when talking to someone they don't like. You will start to see these patterns over time.

Once you get a handle on these patterns, you can start to adjust.

Point 2 Find the Omens

The omens of anger can be felt via gestures and the words one uses. This may include things like narrowing one's eyes or nervously touching hair or glasses.

This behavior varies by person, but nonetheless, such verbal and physical indicators come out unconsciously when people feel anger rising. These can be identified via daily observation.

If you see these omens, try to distract the person from their object of anger.

Point 3 Avoid Land Mines

There is an expression in Japanese, "gekirin ni fureru," which means something similar to "stepping on a landmine." "Gekirin" means "a scale that grows in backwards on a dragon's chin." The word comes from a legend in which a dragon has a "gekirin" and kills anyone who touches it. The expression refers to infuriating someone based on something you do.

By avoiding behaviors and words that people with intense anger don't want "touched," you can avoid conflicts.

2 | Anger Duration

Try to evaluate the duration of your anger according to the 10-point scale below.

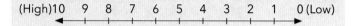

(High)10   9   8   7   6   5   4   3   2   1   0 (Low)

Anger "duration" is an index that quantifies how much time you tend to spend feeling angry.

When anger persists for a long time, it may not even end with a single person's life. Anger can be passed down from generation to generation, like in religious and ethnic conflicts. The behavior of stalkers can be described in terms of lingering resentment at a person of interest not behaving the way one wants as well.

People all have different lengths to their anger. Some people can get incredibly angry and then are fine once they let it out, while other people can't bring themselves to let something go no matter how long they stay mad.

People with high anger duration are people with good memories and excellent concentration. They build up their anger slowly and return to it again and again in memory. However, as this goes on, their feelings of anger become warped and can amplify other unpleasant feelings, like anxiety.

Even people with middling anger duration have memories of anger that they find hard to forget. As long as they are engulfed by that angry feeling, they will continue to relive it unnecessarily, and it becomes difficult to think constructively about the future.

"A bamboo-splitting personality" is an expression in Japanese which refers to people who can let out all their anger in a flash and then act as though nothing happened at all. People with low anger duration are like this.

People with long-lasting anger have the following characteristics:
- Perfectionists with lots of pride
- Sensitive and meticulous
- Constantly thinking and often in their own world

People with long-lasting anger usually seem to be calm and composed at a glance, but have a very emotional interior. This kind of person can suddenly become angry. What's more, the origin of the anger can be things long in the past or trivial daily matters, which can come as quite a surprise to the target of the anger. However, this is also evidence that the person is usually trying to endure their anger and not take it out on others.

A Prescription for Your Anger

People with long-lasting anger are often people with a tendency to overthink things. When their anger continues, they aren't only thinking about the present – they are thinking about the past, the future, and other situations.

The past refers to the cause of anger, while the future may involve thinking about retaliation. All these things are things that don't exist in the present.

Try to think only about what exists in the present, right in front of you.

It's true that your painful experiences are a part of you, but it is important to ensure that they don't act as shackles preventing you from living a happy, enjoyable life.

It's a bit trite to say it, but the truth is you can't change the past or other people. Don't let your persisting anger cause you to suffer.

Let's take a look at some methods to help you avoid overthinking things.

Method 1 | Live using your dominant and non-dominant hand

One thing you can do to calm your mind is to practice "living by your dominant hand and non-dominant hand."

Of course, you have no problem using a fork or knife or brushing your teeth when using your dominant hand, but if you use your other hand, it requires a lot of concentration. When you focus on something, you lose space for thinking about unnecessary things.

If you use your non-dominant hand to eat, turn over fried eggs, brush your molars, etc., you'll have to focus on what you're doing in the moment without getting lost in your thoughts.

It would be difficult to keep this up from morning until night, so make a determination to do it for 5-10 minutes a day. After doing this enough, you'll start to get a feel for "focusing on the present moment."

Method 2 | Meditate while walking

Meditation is something you can do while you walk. Concentrate on the bottom of your foot. How does it contact the pavement? How does it move ahead of you? Focus on the movement of your left and right side.

It's said that people get most carried away in their thoughts while walking. It's difficult to meditate as you walk all day, so decide instead to meditate on a 10-minute walk, or for the 2 minutes you spend waiting at traffic lights on your commute to work.

"Mindfulness" has become a very popular buzzword. In fact, both the hand technique and this walking technique are ways of practicing mindfulness.

Mindfulness is also known as a stress reduction method, but its original purpose was for reducing anxiety-related mental and physical tension by focusing on the present moment. It is effective for controlling anger for the same reason.

How to Interact with People with Long-Lasting Anger

People with long-lasting anger have a sensitive side and are constantly concerned about how others view them. They are sensitive to criticism, but are unable to show people that they have been hurt.

This is, of course, because they care about their image. They don't want those around them to hate them or lose faith in them. Yet, in doing this, they stockpile anger that eventually explodes.

In order to communicate with someone who stays angry for a long time, keep the following three points in mind.

Point 1 Don't interrupt them

If you butt in with your opinion or point out something that's wrong to this type of person, they'll stew over it no matter how small it is, which builds every time you do it and causes resentment.

Wait for them to finish speaking before saying what you want to say. If possible, don't deny what they are saying, but instead gently say, "Yeah, you're right. I also think you can look at it like this."

Point 2   Sympathize with their Anger

When babies get angry or cry, you may have seen their mother say to them, "Oh, you're angry, aren't you?" or "You're sad, aren't you?" "It's hard, isn't it?" They give words to their child's feelings as they pat them on the back.

People whose anger lasts respond well to this kind of intimate approach. If you think they are upset, sympathize with their feelings before they explode.

Point 3   Give them the option of saying no

People with long-lasting anger tend to be kind and have a hard time saying no. Afterwards, they get angry and say how difficult x or y thing was for them.

Whether you are a boss giving overtime or someone inviting someone you like on a date, first create an environment for them that lets them be honest by giving them the option of saying no.

3 | Anger Frequency

Try to evaluate the frequency of your anger using the 10-point scale below.

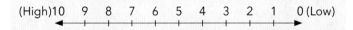

(High)10   9   8   7   6   5   4   3   2   1   0 (Low)

"Anger frequency" refers to how often someone gets upset. When in situations where they keep bumping into things that bother them, the frequency of their anger increases.

On the other hand, people with infrequent anger are able to ignore unpleasant things by saying they aren't a big deal.

Anyone is able to overlook other people's mistakes when they are feeling generous, but when irritated, even small mistakes can set someone off.

Watching a scandal about a celebrity you don't like and feeling indignant, rolling your eyes, also falls into the category of getting angry.

People who frequently get angry are always at the end of their emotional ropes and can get triggered by the things they say and hear.

When that happens, some people will raise their voice and make angry faces, but other people will just sit with their feelings.

People whose anger is of a middling frequency will sometimes get angry, sometimes not get angry. They have a wide range of moods, and may be seen as moody by the people around them.

People who infrequently get angry don't really get frustrated or snap at all. However, they may just not be aware of their feelings.

People with frequent anger have the following characteristics:
- Impatience
- Strict with others
- Not very flexible

People who frequently get angry have a strong desire to communicate their feelings. Out of an uncertainty if others understand them, they express their anger by raising their voice and making extreme facial expressions.

A Prescription for Your Anger

First, learn to separate the things that concern you and things that don't concern you, and make an effort to ignore the things that don't concern you.

Method Prepare ways to relax

If you aren't able to change things up, you'll only get more and more irritated. Try to come up with some ways to modify your mood that you can deploy in a variety of situations.

For example, you can think of things to do on the weekend, things you can do on half-days, things you can do during your commute, things you can do while doing housework, things you can do at the office, etc.

It's good to come up with some variation for your relaxation methods. If you make a decision to do something, it doesn't work out, and you don't have a back-up plan, you'll just get even more upset. I recommend activities that help release your physical tension in order to relax. This might include taking walks, baths, stretching, or reading books.

On the other hand, drinking alcohol or eating out of despair is no good. If you just keep drinking, or eating when you aren't hungry, you'll give yourself new stress rather than calming yourself down.

How to Interact with People with Frequent Anger

When people become yes-men out of fear of reprisal, their frustration will only rise.

I recommend dealing with this anger type based on the following three points.

Point 1 Temporarily humor them without objection

Directly contradicting a prideful person who often gets angry will just add fuel to the fire.

If the person is a client or supervisor and it seems that giving a contrary opinion may result in you getting raked over the coals, just agree with them temporarily and set up a later time at which you can try to negotiate with them calmly.

Point 2 Perfect your Ho-Ren-So

Because uncertainty can result in anger, get your Ho-Ren-So practices down.

If the person you are talking to is easily angered, you may feel that they are difficult to engage. If that's the case, just write a memo, e-mail, or send them an instant message.

Point 3 Make a point of agreeing

It's natural for someone to try harder to get their point across if they're doing their best to explain something and they aren't getting a reaction out of their audience.

Say "yes" or nod in a visible way to politely show that you are listening and understand what is being said to you to keep things going smoothly.

4 | Anger Resistance

Try to evaluate your anger resistance
using the 10-point scale below.

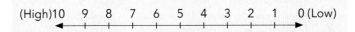

(High)10   9   8   7   6   5   4   3   2   1   0 (Low)

"Anger resistance" is an index of how easily you are angered.

People who easily get angry aren't good at dealing with people getting angry with them, while people who don't get angry easily are.

This "Resistance" is an item which requires more caution the *lower* the score.

People with low anger resistance are not good at accepting ways of looking at things that differ from their own. For that reason, they often collide with the people around them.

Even if you can't give a full inch, try to give at least half an inch. Even if something doesn't receive a perfect 100 in your book, it's important to be able to accept a score of 70 or 50.

People with middling resistance sometimes find themselves unable to tolerate the views of others. Try to assign a score – 100, 70, 50 – to quantify whether or not you are unable to accept something, and to what extent.

People with high resistance, on the other hand, are able to take things and the conduct of others in stride. Of course, that doesn't mean that they can accept anything.

Letting things you disagree with go because it's hard to speak up may be bad for your self-confidence, so take care on this point.

People with low resistance to anger have the following characteristics:
- Sensitive and emotional
- Self-confidence and firm beliefs
- Often says things like "it's for your sake."

A Prescription for Your Anger

People with low anger resistance have a small tolerance window for people and things. As a result, they have a hard time accepting perspectives that differ from theirs. They often have extreme views and are always trying to determine if others agree with them or not.

Everyone has their own perspective on things. Society is possible because of our different views. If everyone thought the same things as you and wanted to do the same things as you, civilization would cease to function.

Try to accept other viewpoints. When you do so, don't evaluate those viewpoints as either 0 or 100, but determine if they are 50% similar to you, 70% similar to you. Try to see what parts are the same as you.

By doing so, you can increase your tolerance towards people and things, and your resistance to anger will rise.

Method Increase your tolerance, little by little

People have different expectations even when it comes to things like greetings.

Some people won't recognize a greeting unless you loudly say "Good morning!" to them, while others are fine with a more casual nod. Some people are fine with just eye contact.

A loud "Good morning!" might be 100 points, while a nod is 70 points. Try seeing the nod as fitting into a category of "greeted me."

If eye contact gets 30 points, it may not be within your range of tolerance – but it's not like they ignored you completely!

Thinking in this way will enable you to accept the greetings of others that you previously wouldn't recognize as a greeting at all.

How to Interact with People with Low Anger Resistance

People with low anger resistance are often self-confident yet also sensitive. Because of this, if someone goes at them with emotional complaints over something minor, they respond in kind and the conversation devolves into an argument.

Acting with these three points in mind may prove effective.

Point 1 Rather than question, be taught

Casual questions can be interpreted by this type as an interrogation, which can upset them.

Try adding phrases like "Could you teach me?" or "If you know" or "What do you think?"

Point 2 Start with your conclusion

This type is not good at listening to long stories. Try to start what you want to say with the point you want to make.
Trying to preface what you want to say in an effort to be polite can actually just annoy this type.

Point 3 Don't engage in bad flattery

People with low anger resistance don't hate being praised by others. However, if they get praised for obvious things, they may think that you're suggesting that they're barely capable of even doing that much, or that you're looking down on them, and get upset. Being too considerate in this way can backfire.

5 | Anger Aggressiveness

This diagnostic looks at where and how anger is wielded. When anger is difficult to control, it can end up being directed at targets in powerful, violent ways.

Those targets can be split into 3 categories: "people," "oneself," "things."

Try to self-evaluate the aggressiveness of your anger on a 10-point scale.

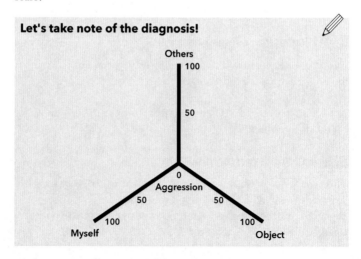

Let's take note of the diagnosis!

Others
100

50

0
Aggression

50   50

100   100

Myself   Object

People

This category concerns the tendency to direct anger at people other than oneself. Typically, other people are blamed in angry moments. When aggressiveness is directed at people, conflicts will frequently arise, people will keep a distance from the angry person, and it becomes difficult to maintain healthy relationships.

Oneself

This category concerns the tendency to direct anger at oneself. In other words, one tends to blame oneself. Repeated self-blame causes anger to build up and results in a loss of self-confidence.

Things

This category concerns the tendency to direct anger at things. In other words, breaking things or acting violently with the environment. Rather than taking anger out on things, find the courage to face what you must face.

As an emotion, anger comes with more energy and passion than any other. When that energy is expressed aggressively and directed at a variety of targets, it can lead to destructive behavior that harms people and things.

However, that doesn't mean that anger always has to result in aggressiveness. Feelings of "What the hell!" and "You'll pay for this!" can instead be channeled into succeeding with the tasks that lay before you.

People who tend to direct anger at others

- Strong defensive instinct

Even if people nearby aren't the true source of anxiety or fear, they get used as stand-ins. The result is what looks like a stereotypical outburst of anger. This angry energy is directed at family or employees – in other words, at people the angry person expects will forgive them for their behavior.

People who tend to direct anger at themselves

- Good people with feelings of guilt

This type tends to be serious, passionate about everything, and feel an unusually strong sense of responsibility and duty. Because they believe that getting angry with others is wrong, they have a hard time expressing anger.

With nowhere to go, their anger gets directed inwards. They are tormented by a feeling of helplessness and lose their positivity. Eventually this can even lead to health issues and susceptibility to sickness.

People who tend to direct anger at things

- Usually kind and patient

When this type snaps, they can suddenly throw and break things around them in an effort to relieve stress. They can be a bit childish and can't express their anger verbally, so they reflexively take it out on their environment.

Method Create some distance from targets of anger

People who direct their anger at people and things can try to pour those feelings into something they like – whether it's sports, a hobby, whatever.

In order to prevent angry feelings from monopolizing your mood, make sure to have some relax time that creates physical and mental distance from anger targets.

How to Interact with People with High Anger Aggressiveness

In general, kind and serious people make for good targets of anger outbursts. This is because they will endure even irrational treatment without complaint. People who react in exactly the desired way also make for prime targets.

Point 1 Don't try to fight back

No matter how logically you try to speak with someone who is immersed in an effort to vent their anger, you'll only add fuel to the fire. When you're speaking to someone above you, they may just interpret whatever you say as backtalk and attack you even more.

In this case, it's better to emotionally distance yourself from the situation and simply agree until they tire themselves out.

Point 2 Leave the area

If you start to feel a storm brewing, just get out of there. You are under no obligation to pointlessly endure a tirade that has nothing to do with you.

The thing to do is avoid contact. Make an excuse, like needing to go to the restroom, and leave the vicinity to avoid getting held up. If you go back 5 minutes later, things will probably have settled down more than you might expect.

Point 3 Prioritize yourself and express your feelings

This is the last resort if methods 1 and 2 don't seem to be working. Tell the person directly how much they are scaring the people around them with their mean-spirited words and violent behavior.

Do this without blaming them, but by flatly telling them that you find them scary. In this way, you prioritize yourself and communicate your feelings without attacking.

Chapter 4

A 21-Day Constitution Training Program to Learn Anger Management

Anger Management is "Mentality Training"

In chapter 2, you learned about your anger type and how to deal with it. In chapter 3, you learned about your anger tendencies. Now that you understand your anger tendencies, let's talk about ways in which you can actually learn to control those angry feelings.

The 21-day training regimen that follows aims to turn the principles of anger management into an actionable set of habits. It is 21 days long because that is roughly the amount of time it takes to develop a new habit.

It will all be quite difficult in the beginning, but if you can make it to the end, anger management will be second nature to you. It will be as easy as breathing.

There is something for you to do every day, so if you just follow all the instructions, the three weeks will be over before you know it.

This program consists of 3 categories of activities:

1. Daily Activities:
   Anger Log
   "3 Control Methods" when you feel upset

2. Individual Day Activities:
   Day 1: Miracle Day Exercise, Transformation Log
   Day 7: 3 Column Technique
   Days 8 & 15: Success Log
   Day 14: Should Log

3. Extras for when you're able:
   Week 1: Pattern-breaking
   Week 2: 24-hour "Act Calm"
   Week 3: Roleplay

Keep it up for 21 days while checking what you have to do each day!

Contents of the training on days 1-21

Something I do every day.		The Anger Log, "Three Cyphers" if you're pissed off.	
Week 1	Day 1	Miracle Day * Exercise * Change Log	*(Break pattern).
	Day 2		
	Day 3		
	Day 4		
	Day 5		
	Day 6		
	Day 7	Three-column technique	
Week 2	Day 8	Success log	*(24 hours a day, Actokerm)
	Day 9		
	Day 10		
	Day 11		
	Day 12		
	Day 13		
	Day 14	Binary log	
Week 3	Day 15	Success log	*(Playroll)
	Day 2		
	Day 17		
	Day 18		
	Day 19		
	Day 20		
	Day 21	Miracle Day * Exercise	

*( ) …Try it, If you have some spare time.

1 | **Daily Activities**: Anger Log

The foundation for learning to control anger is the Anger Log.

The Anger Log is a record of all the times you have felt frustrated, mad, or upset. Putting these moments into words is an effective technique for visualizing the contents of your anger.

Feelings of anger can't be seen, and with time, details are forgotten. It can be surprisingly difficult to get a handle on anger. The Anger Log exists to make that easier. By understanding the things that upset you or irritate you on a daily basis, you will become able to manage your feelings of anger.

Further, by getting into the habit of recording your feelings, you will become able to make yourself calm on the spot. Rather than getting reflexively angry, you can momentarily manage that anger by taking memos of your feelings.

A particular welfare institution has made this Anger Log a requirement for all of their employees. This has resulted in a dramatic drop in turnover, an increase in efficient communication, and the quality of the service itself has improved as a result.

Now let's take a look at how to write the Anger Log.
These are the main 3 guidelines:

1. Write entries immediately
2. Write an entry every time you become irritated or upset
3. Don't analyze while you're writing

Apart from following these 3 guidelines, you are free to write your entries however you like. You can write them in a diary or a notebook or your smartphone. You can also send them to yourself as messages in a messenger app, which will record the date and time for you.

*Examples of Anger Log data

1. Date and time of getting angry
2. Location
3. What happened
4. What you thought
5. Anger temperature (10 levels)

While you shouldn't analyze or criticize the contents when writing your Anger Log, review what you've written after you've made entries for a number of days. In so doing, you will be able to objectively understand the tendencies and characteristics of your anger.

1. Date and time	*month, day*
2. Place	*during my morning commute*
3. What happened?	*I still haven't gotten an estimate from X*
4. What did you think?	*Didn't I tell them it was urgent?!*
5. Anger temperature	1 2 3 4 5 6 7 8 9 10

1. Date and time	
2. Place	
3. What happened?	
4. What did you think?	
5. Anger temperature	1 2 3 4 5 6 7 8 9 10

*Anger Log example

1. Date and time	*Date*
2. Place	*Morning commute*
3. What happened?	*Still no estimate from Y*
4. What did you think?	*Didn't I tell them it was urgent?!*
5. Anger temperature	1 2 3 4 5 6⊕ 7 8 9 10

1. Date and time	*Date*
2. Place	*My desk at work*
3. What happened?	*No report from my employee on a task I assigned*
4. What did you think?	*I took a chance giving them some responsibility, maybe that was premature*
5. Anger temperature	1⊕ 2 3 4 5 6 7 8 9 10

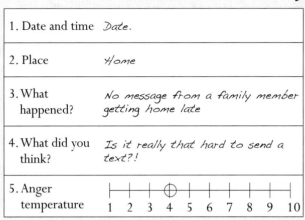

1. Date and time	*Date.*
2. Place	*Home*
3. What happened?	*No message from a family member getting home late*
4. What did you think?	*Is it really that hard to send a text?!*
5. Anger temperature	1 2 3 4 5 6 7 8 9 10

From these logs, the writer may be able to see that slow communication tends to upset them. They might also see from the "What I thought" entries that they feel people should get in contact promptly, and that they can be prone to worrying and impatience.

In the case of this individual, some strategies might include asking family and employees to keep them updated or giving specific deadlines for various tasks, like "Please respond by tomorrow."

In this way, use of the Anger Log enables one to understand one's anger habits and their "should"s. In turn, they will be able to come up with countermeasures, and find ways to avoid needless anger.

2 | "**When you snap**": 3 Types of Control

This is something that is done every time you "snap" during your daily life.

1. Impulse control

When you snap, first wait 6 seconds. This isn't settled science, but it seems that it takes about 6 seconds before anger can be managed rationally. If you can get past those first 6 seconds, you can avoid getting hijacked by your emotions and reflexively getting upset.

So how do you get over those first 6 seconds? Here's a few methods.

What I most recommend is a "coping mantra." This technique uses a phrase that calms you down. When you "snap," immediately start repeating it to yourself in your head.

It doesn't actually matter what the mantra is, but you need to decide what it is in advance. It might be something like, "It's ok, it's ok," or "It doesn't matter, it doesn't matter."

It doesn't even have to be words – you could clench and open your hand or swing your arm. The point is that by doing this repeatedly, you are able to calm yourself down on the spot.

There is also an effective technique called the "Scale Technique." Prepare an image of a thermometer measuring your anger in your heart. When you get angry, give your "anger temperature" a score, like 3 or 5 (see page X)

One reason why we have difficulty controlling our anger is that we don't have a way to measure it. We don't usually compare how angry we were one time to how angry we were another.

For example, if "0" means being completely at peace and "10" means the angriest you've ever been in your life, you might give "I didn't get back that pen I let someone borrow" a 3.

The benefit of assigning points in this way is that it objectifies anger, and putting points to things makes establishing countermeasures possible.

In terms of temperature, what you'll wear will depend on whether it's hot or cold outside. In the same way, if you know your anger temperature, you can adjust your response to your feelings.

By using these techniques, you can learn to redirect your anger from its target. The 6 seconds will be up before you know it.

2. Thought control

If you can manage to avoid reflexively getting angry, draw three circles inside your head. These circles represent the amount of "should" you can allow.

The very center is exactly the same as your "should" – your expectations. It's your ideal outcome, 100%. The circle outside of this isn't quite the same as your ideal, but it is tolerable. The circle on the outside is so different from what you expect that you cannot allow it.

The point of anger management is not to end feelings of anger. It is to enable you to get angry in a productive way when necessary and manage your anger when it is not necessary. It is about understanding the line between the two. These circles are your way of understanding the boundaries.

If you feel angry, ask yourself: in what circle does this belong?

Imagine now that you are upset at a junior colleague who did not greet you.

In this case, consider what sort of situation would fall into the inner circle. For example, this might be something like, "My colleague looks me in the eye and says 'Good morning!' loud enough for me to hear." This is your ideal outcome.

Next, think about the "tolerable" circle. You can identify it using phrases like "at least" or "at minimum."

For example, "At least say 'Good morning,'" or, "At least look towards me and greet me," or, "At a minimum, say something," etc. It's the range of outcomes you can find acceptable.

The more you can expand the size of this second circle, the less you will get upset.

In which zone is the anger in (1) to (3)?

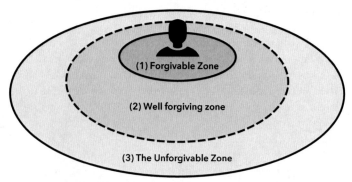

(1) The same "should" as yourself.
(2) It's a little different from what I "should" do, but it's acceptable.
(3) Things that "should" be different from you and are not acceptable.

That said, the idea isn't to allow anything at all with no restrictions. The goal is to better define the boundaries of what you personally can accept and can't accept, and expand them in a way that works for you via training.

3. Behavior control

To say it again, anger management is not about denying your anger. The goal of anger management is to help you identify the times when getting angry is appropriate, and when anger isn't the necessary response.

If you reach stage 3 even after going through the thought control we just discussed, go ahead and get angry.

However, let's talk about how to behave when this happens.

First, make a determination as to whether the thing that is upsetting you is something you have the power to change or not.

For example, consider getting stuck on the train during a delay. You hear the following announcement: "Due to an accident, we will be briefly delayed until we complete a safety check." Surely, there is nothing you could do to change this situation.

Next, determine how important this is.

For example, imagine that you are waiting in line for a taxi and somebody cuts into the line. There are variables that may make things more urgent – it's really cold out, your feet are hurting, etc. – but in general, you can determine that this situation is not that big of a deal.

Following this line of thought, you can divide things that happen into the following 4 categories, arranged in a 2-by-2 grid:

1. I can change it + it's important
2. I can change it + it's not important
3. I can't change it + it's important
4. I can't change it + it's not important

	I can change it I have control	I can't change it I don't have control
It's important	(1) Deal with it now "Until when?" "To what extent?"	(3) Accept the things you cannot change Find a realistic option
It's not important	(2) Deal with it when you can "Until when?" "To what extent?"	(4) Let it be

Then ask yourself: "Where does this thing I'm upset about belong?"

If it's category 1, it's something you need to get started on right away. However, first, determine for how long and to what degree it must be changed for you to be satisfied.

There may be a lot of cases where handling employees or children fall into this area. Often, when a person gets upset when others won't change, it's because that person hasn't made a clear determination of how long and to what extent change must happen to satisfy them.

If it falls into category 2, it's something that you can take up when you have time. You don't need to worry about it immediately.

For example, maybe you get upset in the middle of the night when you recall an e-mail an employee sent you. However, you can't do anything about it in the middle of the night, so it's important to try not to think about it.

Dealing with things in category 3 can be tricky. You have to accept the reality that you can't change things, creating a big emotional hurdle.

For example, what if you get stuck in traffic when you're in a hurry? You can't do anything to break through the jam – but time is of the essence. In these cases, try to accept that you can't do anything about the traffic. Send advance notice, distract yourself with music, or find other things that you can do.

This is also the category to which difficult supervisors belong. Unfortunately, there's probably not much you can do to change your supervisor, so you have to come up with strategies to deal with them.

Finally, items in category 4 should be ignored as much as possible.

For a lot of people, violations of public etiquette likely show up in this category. It may bother you, but endeavoring to not look at or to ignore such things is an important part of learning to deal with anger.

These are the things you should do in your daily life, every day, whenever you get angry. By repeating these "3 methods of control," you will become able to deal with problems without being carried away by anger.

3 | **Day 1 Part 1**: Miracle Day Exercise (setting goals)

The Miracle Day Exercise is about setting goals for your anger management.

This technique helps increase your motivation by imagining a "miracle day" in which you were able to solve your problems with anger management.

First, imagine the day as 21 days from now to make it real, as the culmination of the training program. When you wake up on the morning of the day, the problems you hoped to resolve with anger management have been resolved.

What sort of day is it? The things that once bothered you have astonishingly lost all power over you, people you couldn't stand are now easy to interact with – it's a new you.

Imagine this miracle day, and then answer the following questions.

Try to answer these questions as thoroughly and with as much detail as possible. The more specifics you write down, the clearer your goals will become. This will help clarify your behavior moving forward.

* Miracle Day Exercise entry examples:
* How has your behavior changed? Who notices the change in you first? What do they say?
* Does anyone else notice your transformation?
* What do you personally feel?
* If your Miracle Day is a 10 on a 10-point scale, what other day in the past year has come closest to a 10?
* What did you do on that day? Were you with anyone?

* Miracle Day Exercise entry examples:

* How has your behavior changed? Who notices the change in you first? What do they say?

* Does anyone else notice your transformation?

* What do you personally feel?

* If your Miracle Day is a 10 on a 10-point scale, what other day in the past year has come closest to a 10?

* What did you do on that day? Were you with anyone?

4 | **Day 1 Part 2**: Change Log
(determine what you can do)

Once you have an idea of your goals after the Miracle Day Exercise, the next thing to do is think about what to do to realize them. This is the purpose of the "Change Log."

There is a gap between ideals and reality. Closing that gap helps with realizing your goals.

What must you do to approach your ideal? Imagine what you need to move towards a miracle morning without the stress of angry feelings, and then start laying out the concrete steps you need to take to make it a reality.

These steps could be planned out over time, such as:
- What you can do now
- What you can do by tomorrow
- What you can do in a few days' time
- What you can do in a week's time
- What you'd like to do in the future

I recommend you start on the quick things to build confidence and motivation, moving up to larger and larger tasks.

First, write the steps out and review them. If you assign yourself tasks that are too far removed from your current reality, you'll end up frustrated. It is important to make the steps realistic.

Change Log entry examples

1. Goals to meet
2. Realistic and specific steps needed to realize goals

* Goals to realize	* Realistic and specific steps needed to realize goals *Time needed to perform steps
(Example) *Don't lash out at family*	*(Example)* * *Consciously say "Please" and "Thank you"* * *Put aside time to talk every day* * *Do it for 2 months!*

5 | **Day 7** : 3 Column Technique
(Moving towards core beliefs)

Over the 21 days of this program, at the end of every 7th day is an opportunity to look over the events of the week using a training method called the "3 column technique."

The 3-column technique enables you to identify the "should" lying at the heart of your anger so you can think about what you can do to manage those feelings.

However, you must be cognizant of the timing. Please do not use this technique if you are feeling angry.

Entries in the Anger Log don't require any analysis when writing them, but deep reflection is necessary for the 3 Column Technique. Find a time when you feel calm and are able to think things through when you do it.

Now let's look at how to do the 3 Column Technique.

The columns are essentially boxes. To begin, imagine 3 empty boxes in your mind's eye.

For the first box (column 1), choose one of your entries from the Anger Log from the past week to place inside for analysis. For example, you might write, "I was upset when X showed up 10 minutes late to our meeting."

Next, uncover the "should" behind the anger in the entry you wrote for the first box. Write that down in column 2, putting it in the second box.

For example, the "should" behind getting upset at someone

arriving late might be, "People shouldn't be late to meetings," or, "People should at least get in touch if they're going to be late."

Then, think about how this "should" is able to promote the happiness of the people around you and yourself long-term. Write your thoughts in the third column, for the third box.

This technique is called "reframing," as it reconstructs the "frame" of your "should" – the way you see it.

3 Column Technique example

Column 1: There was an error in the specifications we received so all the work we've done until now is a wash.

Column 2: The side making the order should check things more carefully before we start work.

Column 3: Maybe the person overseeing it was busy.

It would have been better if this had been discovered before we finished the work. Maybe this is a good opportunity to implement a preliminary check system.

What is important here is noticing that this exercise is not about denying your "should."

However, if two sides not compromising on their "should" leads to anger and unpleasant feelings, it may be possible to erase that dissatisfaction by reframing the "should" involved.

In the previous example, the person who made the mistake will have to work a lot of overtime to fix it, but if they're panicking about it, they won't be able to focus on their work. By rethinking one's "should," it will be easier to approach the issue with a different attitude.

It's not that these "shoulds" all have to be rewritten. Like the third box shows, if the "should" helps in ensuring the long-term happiness of yourself and others, you don't need to go out of your way to change it.

\<Column 1> Anger Log	*(example)* *I was upset when X showed up 10 minutes late to our meeting.*
\<Column 2> The "should" behind your anger	*(example)* *People shouldn't be late to meetings.*
\<Column 3> How does this "should" ensure the long-term happiness of myself and others?	*(example)* *Even trains can be late sometimes. Maybe 10 minutes isn't such a big deal.*

6 | **Week 1** : Pattern-breaking (as preparatory training)

There are also some activities (preparatory training) that don't need to be done every day for the 21-day program but should be done when you have the time.

Our daily lives are ruled by a vast array of patterns and habits. There are many people who wake up at the same time on weekdays, watch the same news program while getting ready, get on the same train at the same time to commute to work, and check e-mail and go through a variety of sub-routines upon arrival.

The "pattern-breaking" training is a way to change that rhythm up a bit. For example, how about changing the channel and watching a different program in the morning?

It's a small thing, yet you might feel some uncertainty or discomfort in the differences in the announcer's voice, or notice that the weather isn't being displayed in the corner of the screen that it usually is.

People fall into patterns because they are efficient and comfortable. Moving according to a pattern reduces errors and waste and offers peace of mind. It's not a bad thing, but getting too accustomed to these patterns can lead to your field of vision narrowing, a loss of flexibility, and a stiffening of one's thoughts.

Pattern-breaking seeks to change these singular patterns by changing some aspect of them, however small. This can be anything – commute route, fashion, manner of speaking, stores visited, etc. Deliberately trying to change these patterns will increase your ability to be flexible and also increase your ability to deal with sudden stress.

By the end of the first week you should feel used to writing the Anger Log, though it may have been a tiring experience. In order to progress even farther in anger management, give this exercise a try.

* List of patterns	*What to change?
Example I have bread and coffee for breakfast every day.	– Try rice and miso soup with an omelette – Try a "detox" with a vegetable smoothie

7 | **Days 8 and 15** : Success Log
(review your accomplishments)

The "Success Log" activity is done at the start of the second and third week.

The purpose of this activity is to review your accomplishments. You can look at how well you've accomplished the steps you laid out in the "Transformation Log" or look at things you did that left you with a feeling of success after beginning your training.

Now that you have begun this training, perhaps now you finally feel as though you have reached an understanding of your feelings. Try writing about it in your Success Log. It doesn't matter if it seems like a trivial thing - go ahead and write it.

Success Log examples

- I got angry when someone stepped on my foot, but I waited 6 seconds, and was able to let it go

- I took a deep breath 3 times and felt better

| Accomplishments | *What to change? | | | | |
	Easy				Difficult
(*Example*) I got angry when my boss yelled at me, so I repeated my mantra.	1	2	3	4	5
	1	2	3	4	5
	1	2	3	4	5

8 | **Day 14** : Should Log (facing core beliefs)

After 2 weeks have passed, on day 14 it would be good to do the "Should Log." In this activity, you'll look over your entries in the Anger Log and elsewhere.

What are your "shoulds"? The "Should Log" is a technique to help you see them in a new light.

"Should" is, in one sense, the source of feelings of anger. Therefore, understanding how to face and deal with these "shoulds" is anger management itself.

Once you understand when and in what ways your "shoulds" activate, it will become easy to control them. You can remove yourself from the situation or change your circumstances before exploding in anger, enabling you to guard against it from happening.

- How to write the "Should Log"

1. Write out the "shoulds" and "should nots" that you believe to be true
2. Evaluate how important each of the items you listed in (1) is on a 10-point scale

- "Should Log" example

- People should not talk loudly on the train.   6/10
- People should give advance notice when they are going to be late.   8/10
- If you participate in a meeting you should say something at least once.   7/10

One thing that it is important to keep in mind when facing these "shoulds" is taking the "shoulds" of others as seriously as your own, recognizing how important they are to the people who hold them.

Rather than declaring yourself right and others wrong, consider that there is as much variety to different "shoulds" as there are people in the world.

My "shoulds"	Importance (10-point scale) Low High
(Example) *Meetings should end on time*	1 2 3 4 5 6 7 8 9 10
	1 2 3 4 5 6 7 8 9 10
	1 2 3 4 5 6 7 8 9 10

9 | **Week 2** : 24-hour "Act Calm" (preparatory training)

Week 2's preparatory training is the 24-hour "Act Calm" activity. Add this to your daily training as you are able.

In the 24-hour "Act Calm" exercise, your goal is to remain calm for 24 hours regardless of how you are feeling. If you get angry, if you get irritated – or if you feel sad or depressed – will yourself to only use calm language and behave in a calm manner for a full 24 hours.

We all have a tendency to want others to change rather than change ourselves. Sometimes, we try to achieve this by yelling at, persuading, or otherwise coercing others.

However, in reality, trying to change people who don't want to change is a Herculean task – as they say, "you can't change people or the past."

During your "24-hour Act Calm" period, you will be able to see how things around you change by changing yourself. While you put on a calm face, carefully observe your surroundings.

In so doing, you may come to realize that it is faster and easier to change yourself than to change others.

The more busy you expect to be for your "Act Calm" day, the more effective it will be. The more contact you will have with others, the more value there will be in this activity.

10 | **Week 3**: Role-playing (preparatory training)

The role-playing activity is preparatory training done in week 3. In this activity, you will attempt to play the role of your ideal person.

Your ideal person can be anyone. It can be someone you're close to – your boss, your senior colleague, or just an image of the kind of person you want to become. It could also be a historical figure or a character from a movie or novel.

"What would that person do in this situation?"

By asking yourself this continuously and acting out the answers you produce, you can bring yourself closer to your ideal. If you aren't sure what you should do in some situation, try doing more research into the personality, speech, mannerisms, and story of the individual you have chosen. This way your performance will improve, and this ideal will become your own.

If, as a result of this roleplay, you find yourself thinking that the ideal isn't what you expected, you are always free to change your role model.

*Role-playing example

- Role model: A talented surgeon from a drama
--> After imitating this character's confident attitude and
    language, I feel a little more confident too

- Role model: A supervisor respected by their employees
--> I was determined not to lose to my boss who works harder
    than anyone, and I was praised

Anger Management 21-Day Training Calendar

Week One	Date			
	Day	1	2	3
	Things to do	☐ 3 Codes ☐ Anger Log ☐ Miracle Day Exercise ☐ Transformation Log	☐ 3 Codes ☐ Anger Log	☐ 3 Codes ☐ Anger Log
	Other Plans			
Week Two	Date			
	Day	8	9	10
	Things to do	☐ 3 Codes ☐ Anger Log ☐ Success Log	☐ 3 Codes ☐ Anger Log	☐ 3 Codes ☐ Anger Log
	Other Plans			
Week Three	Date			
	Day	15	16	17
	Things to do	☐ 3 Codes ☐ Anger Log ☐ Success Log	☐ 3 Codes ☐ Anger Log	☐ 3 Codes ☐ Anger Log
	Other Plans			

Congratulations! You are now a person who can manage their anger!

4	5	6	7
☐ 3 Codes ☐ Anger Log	☐ 3 Codes ☐ Anger Log	☐ 3 Codes ☐ Anger Log	☐ 3 Codes ☐ Anger Log ☐ 3 Column Technique (☐ Pattern- breaking)

11	12	13	14
☐ 3 Codes ☐ Anger Log	☐ 3 Codes ☐ Anger Log	☐ 3 Codes ☐ Anger Log	☐ 3 Codes ☐ Anger Log ☐ Should Log (☐ 24-hour "Act Calm")

18	19	20	21
☐ 3 Codes ☐ Anger Log	☐ 3 Codes ☐ Anger Log	☐ 3 Codes ☐ Anger Log	☐ 3 Codes ☐ Anger Log ☐ Miracle Day Exercise (☐ Role- playing)

Together, let us move forward free of the chains of rage!